Fossa

by Julie Murray

Abdo Kids UNUSUAL ANIMALS

Abdo Kids Jumbo is an Imprint of Abdo Kids
abdobooks.com

abdobooks.com

Published by Abdo Kids, a division of ABDO, P.O. Box 398166, Minneapolis, Minnesota 55439.

Abdo Kids Jumbo™ is a trademark and logo of Abdo Kids.

Printed in the United States of America, North Mankato, Minnesota.

102024

012025

THIS BOOK CONTAINS RECYCLED MATERIALS

Photo Credits: Alamy, Getty Images, Minden Pictures, Shutterstock, ©Nathan Rupert p15,p19 / CC BY-NC-ND 4.0

Production Contributors: Teddy Borth, Jennie Forsberg, Grace Hansen
Design Contributors: Victoria Bates, Candice Keimig

Library of Congress Control Number: 2024936633

Publisher's Cataloging-in-Publication Data

Names: Murray, Julie, author.

Title: Fossa / by Julie Murray

Description: Minneapolis, Minnesota : Abdo Kids, 2025 | Series: Unusual animals | Includes online resources and index.

Identifiers: ISBN 9798384903048 (lib. bdg.) | ISBN 9798384903741 (ebook) | ISBN 9798384904090 (Read-to-me ebook)

Subjects: LCSH: Fossa (Mammals)--Juvenile literature. | Wildcat--Juvenile literature. | Carnivores--Juvenile literature. | Rain forest animals--Juvenile literature. | Wildlife--Juvenile literature. | Enigmas--Juvenile literature.

Classification: DDC 599.755--dc23

Table of Contents

Fossa

The fossa is a mammal that is found in the forests of Madagascar. There are about 2,500 fossa left in the wild.

Africa
Madagascar
N
E
S
W

The fossa is an unusual animal. It shares features with cats, dogs, monkeys, and weasels. But it is actually related to the mongoose.

Mongoose

Body

Fossas can reach 6 feet (1.8 m) long from head to tail. Their tails make up half of their length! They can weigh about 20 pounds (9.1 kg).

The fossa has a reddish-brown coat. It has paws with retractable claws like those of a cat. It has a dog-like **muzzle** and round ears like a weasel.

The fossa is a good climber. Its sharp claws allow it to climb trees with ease. Its monkey-like tail helps it balance as it climbs and leaps.

Food

Fossas are **agile** hunters. They can run up to 35 miles per hour (56.3 kph)! They use their strong forearms and claws to catch their **prey**.

Fossas eat all kinds of animals. They hunt birds, fish, and small mammals. However, their main source of food is lemurs.

Lemur

Baby Fossas

Female fossas give birth in a **den**. The den can be underground or in a hollow tree. Usually, 2 to 3 pups are born at a time.

Pups are born helpless. They stay in the **den** for months with their mother. They **mature** when they are 2 years old.

More Facts

- Fossas spend most of their time alone. They come together when they are ready to have young.

- Fossas have no natural **predators**. Their biggest threat is the loss of their habitat.

- Fossas can climb headfirst down trees!

Glossary

agile - moving quickly and gracefully.

den - the resting place of wild animals.

mature - come to full or complete physical development.

muzzle - the part of the head of some animals that contains the nose, jaws, and mouth.

predator - an animal that hunts other animals for food.

prey - an animal that is hunted by another animal for food.

Index